Affiliate

The Complete Guide to Affiliate
Marketing (How to Make Money Online
Selling Other People's Products)

Table of Contents

Chapter 1: Decoding Affiliate Marketing – Introduction 5

Chapter 2: 11 Mistakes Affiliate Marketers Make to Kill Their Business 15

Chapter 3: How to Pick Profitable Affiliate Marketing Niches 25

Chapter 4: Step by Step Guide for Creating an Affiliate Marketing Blog 34

Chapter 5: 13 Proven Tips for Improving Your Affiliate Conversions 39

Chapter 6: How to Pick Profitable Affiliate Offers 52

Chapter 7: Fool-Proof Ways for Promoting Affiliate Offers 61

Chapter 8: List Building Secrets Marketers Don't Want You to Know 74

Chapter 9: Search Engine Optimizing Your Affiliate Marketing Posts 79

Conclusion 84

Chapter 1: Decoding Affiliate Marketing – Introduction

What is Affiliate Marketing?

Affiliate marketing is one of the oldest online revenue models that transformed thousands of aspiring marketers into super-power web entrepreneurs. The ingenuity of affiliate marketing as a business model lies in its simplicity, versatility, and sustenance. It is an uncomplicated yet effective way of making money online without having your own products or services. The fact that you do not have to offer specialized services or maintain a vast product inventory makes this an irresistible proposition for several beginner web marketers.

Imagine having an information center at the heart of your town, where people constantly come seeking for information. Whenever locals or tourists need to know anything about the town, they make headway for the center. Now, the local shops and businesses see that you have a targeted information center bang in the middle of the town that has a lot of potential and real information seekers. They decide you can be an additional channel for them to market their services, and thus achieve greater business penetration.

You become their partner. Whenever people come to you to seek information about the town's products and services, you lead them to the store/business that can best meet their needs. Each time they perform an action (buy from the store), you get a nice commission for recommending the store's services or products to your information-seekers. It's really as simple as that.

This is exactly how it works in the virtual world too. You have a wonderful travel site/blog that gives people information about taking cruises around the world. There are reviews of different cruises, information about top things visitors can do at call ports and more. A cruise company decides your reader base is the exact audience they are looking for – cruise fanatics of those looking around to take a cruise.

You sign up to be their affiliate partner and promote their cruises on your web pages with an affiliate link that leads people to their business site. Each time they book themselves on the company's cruise, you get rewarded with a commission. Again, easy peasy?

Again, there's an author-entrepreneur who has written a comprehensive travel guide eBook to the Caribbean region, which can give your target audience a whole lot of information about Caribbean destinations to facilitate a better travel experience. Wouldn't you love that too? You sign up as an affiliate partner for the eBook and each time one of your reader purchases the book from your unique affiliate link, you earn a commission. Who wins here? Literally everyone.

The reader the gets the information he's been scouring the net feverishly for. The business gets a whole lot of new and targeted customers, who would've been difficult to capture otherwise. And best of all – you earn money for simply pitching someone else's products and services to their audience, without having to bother about creating your own.

Buyers do not have to physically visit the merchant's or retailer's store to avail of their products or services. They can buy products/services from the convenience of their homes.

You don't have any products or services of your own. You aren't running the cruise company or writing the eBook. You are simply introducing it to prospective customers who you think may be interested in it. The business gains, the customer gains and ultimately when both gain, you gain too.

Think of affiliate marketing as a virtual real estate business. The real estate professional doesn't offer his homes for rent or sale. They belong to a third people. He/she merely brings the two parties together to complete the sale and earns a commission out of it. It helps the two parties get what they want, and the agent earns his money behind every completed deal/agreement. All he/she does is promotes the listed properties to prospective buyers, without owning any of them.

8 Super Advantages of the Affiliate Marketing Model

1. Low Cost and Risk

One of the biggest advantages of affiliate marketing as a business model is that it requires low set-up or start-up costs compared to other traditional businesses or even online enterprises. The cost of selling other people's products and services is considerably lower that creating your own.

Imagine the cost of research, tweaking, experimenting, promoting or purchasing raw material for your own products or services. It adds up quickly, without the guarantee of profitable returns.

To start any traditional business, you'll need massive upfront capital investment in terms of renting a space, hiring employees, paying overheads (utility bills), and keeping an inventory (that runs into several hundred dollars) ready.

Cut to the chase; an affiliate marketing business can be launched for the cost of a single meal at a café.

You aren't investing in rentals, heavy utility overheads, product inventory, warehouse costs or employee wages. All you need is a website/blog with a registered domain name and hosting, along with some free or optional paid promotional tools.

As a web publisher, you haven't created a very investment intensive business, which means there's not much to lose. Also, it is easy to change from one affiliate program to another if you find something isn't working as anticipated. Experimenting and tweaking become easy when there's little investment involved. All you need to do is quit one affiliate program and sign up for another.

Plus, it can be started within no time. You can literally be in business within 24 hours from now.

2. One Man Army

You don't need a hundred different people to manage various departments of your business, unless you choose to outsource, of course! A majority of the tasks can very well be handled by you, thus eliminating the need to invest your time and energy in people management and office politics.

3. No Need to Reinvent the System

You don't need to do anything path-breaking or reinvent the wheel to make it big in the world of online business. All the systems are in place for you to follow a proven business model of selling others' products and services. There's zero hassle of creating your own unique products or services.

A majority of credible affiliate merchants or businesses provide affiliate partners with a set of ready marketing resources to go out there and promote their business.

4. Sheer Variety

The sheer variety of goods and services you can promote on your blog is staggering. For instance, in the above example of a blog dedicated to cruising, you can promote everything from cruise packages to backpacks to guide books to swimwear.

You can pick and choose from several products/services to be marketed on your blog depending on factors such as commission rates offered or your personal interests. There's just no limit to what you can market on a related blog/website.

5. Zero Expert Knowledge Required

You don't need highly specialized or expert knowledge in the field/niche to sell someone else's products or services. The key is bringing the right products to the right target market by studying your audience trends and behavior.

You have to identify the most compelling needs of your target audience and promote the right merchant offers/products to them, without actually being in possession of specialized/expert knowledge about the domain. Knowing the pulse of your audience is one of the most important aspects of being an affiliate marketer.

6. Source of Passive Income

Passive income is nothing but creating a business once and earning from it several times over in future, sometimes for a lifetime. So, you write a book once and earn royalties on it forever or purchase a property once and keep earning rent from it for as long as you wish, without having to perform any real task to make that money.

Similarly, affiliate marketing is a great source of online passive income. You can set-up your blog/website once by creating awesome content, attention-grabbing visuals, and valuable infographics or videos.

You can earn money consistently from the blog/website each time someone clicks on your link to purchase products/services from you without you having to actually do anything much apart from maybe minor updates to the site periodically. It's almost a one-time setup thing that requires minimal effort once you have a steady stream of traffic eagerly interested in the products/services offered by the affiliate merchants.

You are working once on setting everything up and getting paid for the same task multiple times, every time someone buys through your link.

7. Flexible Hours

The reason thousands of web entrepreneurs are lured by the prospect of affiliate marketing is that it offers a flexible work life that allows you to work from anywhere and anytime you please. You could be earning from a mountain resort in Bali or a beach on the Caribbean for all anyone cares. The business isn't location or time-bound.

Affiliate marketers have the flexibility of pursuing other businesses, further education or a life on the move along with the affiliate business model. Unlike traditional jobs and businesses, you aren't locked into a rigid schedule as long as you devote a few hours to the business each week/month. Many affiliate marketers are location independent and often keep changing their place of residence to experience living in different destinations.

Affiliate marketers can keep their present business or job and still build a profitable revenue generating online system to supplement their current income. Armed with a computer, an internet connection, you can go about creating a rewarding revenue source.

You can literally generate profits 24/7 from just about anywhere in the world. In a nutshell – you are your own boss. You determine your schedule, work hours, location and business strategy. Incredibly cool? You bet!

Since you aren't operating a physical store as a blog/website publisher, you aren't dependent on buyers walking into your store at specific hours. The entire world is your marketplace. Your audience can be anywhere from New York City to Timbuktu and can access your blog/website anytime during the day to offer you money making opportunities without geographical or time limitations. Your shop, so to say, is open all the time for just about everyone in the world.

8. No Customer Support Required

Affiliate partners do not have to put up with the headache of customer or after sales support. There's little need for knowledge of technical support or other customer service related to the product.

Once the sale is complete, all the after sales are handled by the merchant. The merchant is completely in charge of providing support, issuing refunds and answering questions related to the product. Though it helps to know more about the product/service you're selling, you aren't bound to offer it to customers. All you need to concentrate on is promoting and reselling the product or service.

You also don't have to stress about inventory control, order processing, shipping and processing payments/invoicing as an affiliate marketer. All of these operational tasks are handled by the merchant, while you enjoy a slice of the profits.

One of the most significant benefits of affiliate marketing is that affiliate partners or publishers receive top notch support from the merchants in the form of effective ads and updated marketing literature to help optimize profits for both.

Some larger affiliate programs also give you access to the support of a dedicated affiliate manager, who can discuss your individual requirements, and offer helpful pointers for maximizing your profits. Thus merchants are willing to go all out to offer their affiliate partners the best resources since, at the end of the day, it benefits them too.

Disadvantages of Affiliate Marketing

1. Low Commission Rates

Many merchants offer low commission rates that are just not worth it unless you are helping sell a high volume of products/services, which is again a tough proposition. Commission rates vary from program to program depending on several factors. However, on an average, popular brands usually offer low commissions that more often than not do not cover the costs of the affiliates.

The best way to beat this is to find reputable products with high commission rates or the big ticket buys as they are referred to in internet marketing parlance. Even better is to find products/services with recurring commissions. For instance, a subscription or membership based service where the customer is required to renew their commitment to the merchant periodically, and you earn a commission consistently (each time he/she renews their commitment) for getting them to sign up with the merchant just once. Keep hunting for products/services with higher commissions, and various ways to promote those to your target audience.

Strangely, sometimes even something as simple as signing up for the same affiliate program on another marketplace (portal offering several affiliate programs that marketers can pick from, e.g. ClickBank) can boost your commission considerably. So make sure to check the offer on multiple marketplaces before signing up for the one offering the highest commission.

2. Fierce Competition

Affiliate marketing is a fiercely competitive online making domain in virtually every niche/topic that attracts a fair share of demand.

Weight loss, travel, pets, beauty, relationships, making money – virtually every topic is dominated by the big players who gained the early entry advantage. There's a workaround to this too, which we'll discuss during the course of the book. However, it is safe to say that one of the biggest disadvantages of affiliate marketing is the near saturation it suffers from.

There are several affiliate marketers zealously promoting products and services in every conceivable niche. You'll need to extremely creative and resourceful to survive in the world of affiliate marketing, which isn't going to be tough since I've got your back here.

3. Unethical Merchants

Some unethical and unscrupulous merchants may promise huge commissions only to decrease it later. At times they may simply shut shop and vanish without bothering to pay their partners. Though these are extreme cases, it is worth mentioning as a disadvantage.

The very nature of the internet gives you both flexibility and anonymity, which in turn can breed a lack of accountability. The absence of a physical store means that a merchant can almost vanish overnight.

Stick to affiliate programs that are proven, reputed and have bagged good reviews from other well-known affiliate marketers. Stay away from shady offers that look too good to be true. As a rule of the thumb – if something on the internet looks too good to be true, it often is. Use your discretion while picking products and services. Pose questions to the merchant.

Chapter 2: 11 Mistakes Affiliate Marketers Make to Kill Their Business

Most affiliate marketers start with a single goal in mind – money. The scamper all over the place like confused mice trying every trick they learned in overpriced online courses to start making money. There's no direction and zero planning. And then after they're tired and exhausted, they wonder why they aren't sipping a martini on a Hawaiian beach driving a swanky car as shown in the pictures of their marketing guru.

Truth is – it is very easy to fail as an affiliate marketer with the wrong techniques and approach. Though there's no secret sauce or guaranteed formula for affiliate marketing success, there are proven strategies that can well boost your chances of success and certain mistakes you can avoid to earn a consistently profitable income from affiliate marketing.

Through years of personal experience tweaking and fine tuning the system, I realized there are 10 major mistakes most beginner affiliate marketers make to sabotage their own chances. Here they are, just so you know what to avoid for achieving success as an affiliate marketer.

1. Selling Over Helping People Buy

One of the fastest routes to affiliate marketing 'doomdom' is to shove your products/services down your audience's throats without trying to understand their requirements. One too many affiliate marketers are simply interested in selling their products/services to a hapless audience rather than helping them buy or guiding them into buying the right products/services.

The terms affiliate marketing itself defines your role as a marketer and not a salesperson. Your job is to merely promote/market the right services to your audience rather than trying to hard-sell to them, and eventually, annoy them in the bargain.

If you get too greedy and try to kill the hen that lays a golden egg daily with a single swoop in the hope of gaining several golden eggs, you aren't doing it right.

Don't go overboard with the "Buy This Today" or "Purchase This Right Now". Your readers aren't fools. They recognize when people are genuinely trying to help them by offering valuable recommendations and information that can help them versus blatantly selling to them for profits.

Rather than simply screaming BUY everywhere, try to understand the requirements of your target audience. Try to guide them with comparisons of different products so they know what's best for them. Offer unbiased reviews so they understand why they should or should not invest in a particular product. Rather that blindly listing a product's features, attempt to bring out its benefits.

How can it add value to the lives of your readers? In what way will it make things easier for them? How can it be more useful for your readers than something they are currently using? These things go a long way in convincing people that you are interested in helping them buy rather than simply selling to them.

2. Selling Without Building a Brand

Most successful and credible internet marketers will advise you to build a brand and offer value to your customers to win their trust before they decide to purchase through your affiliate link. Your recommendations, reviews and "buy nows" will have weight only if people can trust you to be a credible source of information related to the niche.

Use different channels, including the social media, for building your authority, influence, and credibility on a domain by offering tremendous value to your target audience. Be prepared to give a lot, in the beginning, to build your brand before expecting to get sales from your audience. People really appreciate when you go out of the way to bring free and valuable information at their fingertips.

One of the biggest mistakes affiliate marketers make at the early stages of their business is to set up a site, write a few articles, throw in a few visuals and wait impatiently for people to buy from them. Sorry to disappoint you, but it doesn't work that way. Focus on building a credible, admirable and dynamic reputation first before expecting people to trust your recommendations with their money. Give as much value and information as you can to inspire their loyalty. Avoid pressurizing them into buying during the initial stages and just focus on understanding their needs and striking a conversation.

3. Promotional Overload

Several greedy affiliate marketers fall into the trap of promoting multiple products and services only to cause severe ad blindness to their readers, who become immune to the several hundred marketing messages clogging their blogs/websites.

Focus on promoting a handful of quality products (not more than 2-3 at a time) that are relevant to your target audience. Don't keep hitting multiple darts in the hope that one of them will hit the bull's eye. Most insecure newbie affiliate marketers pick several products/services with the hope that at least some of them will earn decent commissions.

However, people quickly develop a sort of immunity or blindness to excessive marketing messages. They are unable to tell the difference between valuable and crappy offers and hence bundle everything together as worthless.

Prospective customers are solely interested in useful products that can add value to their life. Don't promote several products or services simultaneously as you will be unable to award enough attention or schedule to every product. This will lead to plunging sales. Concentrate on growing sales not the number of services or products to be promoted.

4. Picking Wrong Affiliate Programs

Not every affiliate marketing program can fit the needs of your audience. Most marketers choose products/service that pay decent affiliate commissions or those that have been successfully tried by other marketers without understanding how it fulfills the requirement of their audience.

You also have to consider factors that benefit you in terms of minimum payout, support, usability and other factors. Select products/services that you can easily promote within your time schedule. Consider if the commission to earn from a particular program is worth the amount of time/effort invested in its pre-sales. You also need to ensure that the product you are promoting is high quality and offers top class support to customers. When a marketer is excited and passionate about promoting a product or service, they are able to offer true benefits to their audience.

Marketing poor quality products and services harms your reputation. Your audience will start viewing you as a peddler of low-quality products, and will simply stop trusting you or buying from you. Remember, when you promote a low-quality product, it is your reputation as publisher/affiliate marketer that is at stake. Your audience doesn't know or care about the merchant. They purchase products/services based on your recommendations, and hence you stand to lose big time if their experience is anything less than satisfactory.

On the other hand, satisfied customers will most likely return for more purchases based on a relationship of faith. They are also likely to recommend your site/blog within their social circle. You aren't just increasing your customer base your new customer list but also retaining existing customers for repeat purchases.

5. No Knowledge of Experience of Products/Services

Obviously, you don't have to do a doctorate in the product or service you're promoting. All you need to be armed with is sufficient information to help your audience make the right choice. Would you really purchase a car from a sales executive who doesn't own a vehicle or knows nothing about a car? Not really.

Some of the best affiliate marketers are those who themselves use their products/services they promote. This gives them a clear, first-hand experience edge over other promoters. Since they've used the product/service, their review or suggestions inspire higher credibility than someone who is merely promoting something for commission.

When you have first-hand experience using the product, you promote it from a different position. People view you as a happy customer endorsing a product or service that has greatly benefited you. You are able to demonstrate how it has actually helped you in a more credible fashion. Readers don't just want exaggerated accounts of a product's features or benefits. They love stories with a personal and human touch.

One of the most powerful persuasion strategies is how you discovered and loved a specific product or service and how it impacted your life. Stay miles away from fabricating or 'making up' stories, and stick to authentic accounts. Add your own positive introductory video while promoting a product or service. Check this out right now rarely works until you give your audience enough reasons to do it.

Though merchants will already have copies of sales letters written by professional copywriters, at the end of the day, people trust and buy from other people.

6. Promoting Without a Blog or Website

Though there are plenty of marketers promoting affiliate offers through their mail lists, social media pages, and paid ad programs, it is strongly recommended that you have a blog or website, especially if you are thinking of affiliate marketing as a long-term revenue generation business.

A blog or website lends your business a sort of identity or credibility. It is like a virtual business card or portfolio that tells people more about your business. Blogs and websites are like brands. They make your brand more identifiable, recognizable and unique. Creating a blog or website is a great way of reaching out to your target audience and building trust.

Once you establish a credible reputation for your blog, it is easy to get people to return every time they are looking for information related to your niche, thus converting them into loyalists. We all know it is easier to sell to people when we win their confidence and loyalty. It is tough to achieve that without a blog or website.

People are less likely to take you seriously if you do not have a strong online presence in the form of a well-written and comprehensive blog or website.

7. Depending On a Single Source of Traffic

If you want to achieve success as an affiliate marketer, never depend on a single traffic source. It can kill your business like a few other blunders. Try and optimize your traffic sources so you can get your target audience from several sources.

In addition, putting all eggs in a single source of traffic is committing hara-kiri. Even one Google update or change in algorithms can shut your affiliate marketing shop overnight. Social media channels may alter their policies to reduce your organic reach. Paid advertising programs may go beyond your budget.

Every traffic source has its pros and cons. Optimize the best of every channel and use it to gather your target audience rather than banking heavily over a single source. Expanding your target audience is crucial to achieving favorable sales conversion figures.

8. Not Investing in Valuable Tools

There's really no enterprise that can help you reap profits without investing in the right support tools. Bloggers and publishers looking to be successful in the affiliate marketing model should consider investing in premium web hosting services, fast loading themes, product review plug-ins, SEO tools (Yoast plugin) and popup domination. This enhances user experiences and streamlines the process for you to expedite your profits.

Keep up-to-date with changing technology, social media trends and the affiliate marketing world to comply with fluctuating industry dynamics. What worked a few months ago may be completely obsolete now. Learning to adapt is one of the most required traits of an online marketer.

9. Innovate

You can't achieve extraordinary results by doing ordinary things. If you want to stand out from other affiliate blogs or offers, make yours extraordinary.

Distinguish your brand from others by offering something unique and innovative. Think of a new format for sharing information. Use angles that have been left untapped by others. Think of unique stories and interesting ways to share your experience with the product.

Several affiliates commit the mistake of copy and pasting marketing material from one source to another without putting their soul into it. It's a cut and dried version of everything they process on the internet on a daily basis. Make the proposition of buying from your excitement for them.

You may have spotted a feature or benefit that few marketers are talking about or thought of different ways to use the product or service. Being an innovator is often the difference between an online business that reaps rich profits and one that struggles to stay afloat.

10. Failing to Track Results

Failing is plan is almost always planning to fail. Similarly, failing to track your results is a sure-fire sign of preparing to fail.

At the end of the day, affiliate marketing is a number game. You don't obviously have to a mathematical wizard. However, knowing your numbers helps in tracking metrics that can boost your affiliate marketing business. When you identify a particular profitability formula or source of traffic, it is easy to ride on it to create a winning business model, and then scale it up to roll in big money.

Another huge blunder that marketers make is not using unique tracking affiliate links on every page. When you close a sale for the merchant, you obviously want to learn which page that sale came from so it is easy to increase your conversions, while growing and scaling campaigns that work well. It will also be easier to get rid of losing turkeys.

Earnings commission is absolutely cool. However, knowing where your commissions originated from is even cooler. It equips you with information to develop and scale future campaigns compared to working arbitrarily on several campaigns without nailing the effective ones.

11. The Hot Products Syndrome

Affiliate marketers, especially newcomers, are so taken in by the prospect of earning lots of profits in the short span of time that they end up chasing every hot product in the market without understanding if the product/service complements their blog or audience requirement. What is popular may not necessarily be right or perfect for your audience.

Choose products that are in-demand but also those that resonate with your typical audience. For instance, if you promote an eBook about luxury Caribbean cruises on a budget traveling or backpacking site, it may not perform well.

Understand the needs, values, goals, fears, aspirations and problems of your audience before promoting offers. Pick products that of interest or value to your readers.

Chapter 3: How to Pick Profitable Affiliate Marketing Niches

I presume if you are reading about affiliate marketing, you are all here to make money online.

You require a focused or niche blog to boost your chances of success with affiliate marketing. You can't just write about anything and everything and expect to attract a focused audience. Affiliate marketing blogs are different from diary or reflection style blogs. They need a clear topic or subject, which has a focused audience. Only then can you promote relevantly and laser targeted offers to them.

Picking profitable niches is central to your success of achieving success in the vast world of affiliate marketing. A majority of affiliate markets do not succeed because they fail to pick the right niche.

So, how to do identify your winners from the lemons? How do you pick an affiliate market niche that has thousands of hungry and eager to buy customers? Here are the top 5 secrets to picking profitable affiliate marketing niches.

1. Pick a Niche You Have Established Expertise In

Being knowledgeable in a niche isn't mandatory, but it helps to position yourself as an authority for building credibility and influence. Sometimes people dive into a niche of which they possess zero knowledge base solely on the money-making criteria.

Beginner online marketers often reveal the tendency to pick topics with high searches in their keyword research over topics that they are competent in. Your audience will be able to tell your lack of competency sooner or later and move to another source possessing expert/detailed knowledge about the niche.

It also helps to combine the niche with your background, education, and experience. For instance, if you've worked for years in the travel and hospitality segment, people are likelier to take your hotel reviews and travel recommendations more seriously than if you have a degree in child psychology.

It all kind of adds to the persona of an expert or influencer, though you can always dabble in niches you have no knowledge of but are willing to learn about.

Pro niche selection tip – Pick a niche that reveals an above average competency and you can increase your chances of standing out among similar blogs.

Take, for instance, you find the weight loss and nutrition niche highly lucrative and jump on the bandwagon like hundreds of marketers without any real knowledge about it, you're simply going to rehash stuff that's already available on the internet without adding your own invaluable inputs.

2. Passion is the Key

This money versus passion debate is tricky. If you aren't passionate about the niche, you won't be able to dedicate hours of time, effort, research and writing to the niche, thus losing interest mid-way and giving up.

Affiliate marketing isn't some get rich quick scheme. It is a long-term business that takes time to reveal results. Until then, it is your passion alone that can sail you through.

However, there's another perspective to this highly stimulating debate. If you don't witness encouraging results by picking profitable niches, you start losing interest even if it's a niche you are passionate about.

On the other hand, if you start witnessing small yet encouraging results, you are propelled to carry on even with a niche you don't have much passion for. You invariably begin to develop an interest in a niche that makes you money.

However, I'll root for a combination here not just to play safe but also because it is one that increases your chances of cracking a winner.

Passion helps you think about a niche from different angles. Even if you are outsourcing content creation, it'll be easier to come up with content ideas and marketing strategies if you connect with the topic at a deeper level.

When you expand on topics and ideas, you can easily rank higher for long tail keywords (three to four or more keyword phrases specifically related to the products or services you are marketing). Lengthier or expanded content garner higher views and higher social media shares.

Your enthusiasm for a topic reveals itself in your content, which eventually has a bearing on website audience metrics such as bounce rate, time spent on the page, pages read per session and more. These are some clinchers that ultimately determine your search engine rankings.

It is also important to come with topics that have a fair share of demand because you aren't creating the content for yourself here. You are creating it to build a business around the topic. There has to be some demand for the topic.

Niche selection is probably the single largest factor holding aspiring marketers from building profitable affiliate marketing blogs. It's like developing those pre-wedding jitters. You don't know if you'll make the right choice and don't want to be stuck with a losing niche for a lifetime.

Get out of this permanent state of inertia by starting with something you have some knowledge and passion for, and that has fairly reasonable demand (more on keyword research later). Passion can kill competition – big time.

3. Follow Profits

We've already established that you are in this for money. If you can combine your expertise with profits, that's unbeatable. Can money be made from your specialized knowledge of a rare dog breed? Start researching on Google to find the profit potential of a niche.

Plenty of ads appearing on a simple Google search show there's reasonable demand for the niche. It's a sign there's monetary value that can be tapped into. If the search throws up plenty of products from Amazon, that's another healthy sign that there's a lot of money to be made selling as an Amazon affiliate.

Get down to the bottom of the financial analysis to gauge your profit potential per affiliate sale. Are you going to sell several hundred low-cost products or few premium value items? For instance, a book about puppy training may bring you a few odd $5-7 in commission, while a course that teaches little-known profitable gambling techniques may help you earn much more. Since your niche is closely tied to the products/services you sell, you must work out the type of products you plan to sell to before finalizing the niche.

For instance, if you decide to go with more high ticket items such as charter planes or luxury resorts, you may want to create a site on luxury travel.

4. Narrow It Down

Narrowing it down helps you dominate sub-niches that have a more targeted or focused audience. It eliminates competition prevalent in bigger niches, and positions you as the authority within the given sub-niche. In short, you're signing up to be a big fish in a small pond rather than a small fish in a large pond.

For instance, if you feel the travel niche is already crowded with too many big players vying for the audience's attention, you can go deep down and pull out a single specialty niche that may not have too many informational resources such as pet travel, gay tourism, volunteer tourism, babymoons and much more.

You can become a one-stop information shop for everything related to that travel sub-niche.

Similarly, if you find the weight loss niche too crowded, you can go narrower with post-pregnancy weight loss or weight loss for seniors or weight loss and nutrition for teens.

This niche selection strategy again helps you target more focused, long tail keywords that are brilliant for affiliate marketing conversions.

Not many realize this but Google suggestions is a great way to unearth profitable sub-niches. For instance, when you type weight loss in the search field, you get a ton of suggestions from Google such as weight loss supplements, weight loss workouts, weight loss diets, weight loss post pregnancy etc. Pick one of these sub-niches and check for their profitability using the keyword research techniques mentioned in the chapter.

5. Look Around

There are plenty of unlikely places where you can hunt for the most profitable niches. Sites such as Quora, Reddit, Yahoo Answers etc. can give you a lot of hints about the most compelling issues people face for which they need quick solutions. Even website marketplaces such as Flippa can be a nice resource for digging niches that work.

Even a simple visit to the local store or magazine stand can give you tons if ideas about specialized niches that people are interested in. There are plenty of special interest periodicals that can act as a great source of inspiration for your niche selection. It's all right there. You just have to sniff around in the right places to scoop out the most profitable niches.

Hell, you can be seated in a café and come up with a niche like smoothies for diabetics.

6. Trends or Evergreen?

This is another raging affiliate marketing trend. While seasoned marketers are constantly looking to cash in on current trends, there are many takers for evergreen niches or niches which never go out of fashion.

Typically trend based niches include topics that are currently hot such technology (probably the latest iPhone), green living, games (Pokemon Go), tiny homes and other major current trends.

Evergreen niches, on the other hand, are those that are forever sought after by the internet audience. Niches related to making money, health, relationships, travel etc are evergreen niches that don't go out of vogue. Irrespective of the conditions around them, people always want more money, good health, more fulfilling relationships and leisure activities.

Hot niches are great if you are targeting quick, seasonal profits. The demand can be at its peak. However, audience interest can gradually fade once the niche goes out of trend. With an evergreen niche, you can continue building your business for years.

Some people like to launch a ton of hot niche sites, make profits and shut shop before moving to the next happening niche, while others stick to an evergreen authority blog and work on building it as a long-term business.

7. Gold is in the Research

Keyword research can be both – tedious and fun. You can play with multiple niches and keywords, dig out for topic ideas and come with a ton of content creation inspiration.

Start with a free keyword tool such as Google's Keyword Tool. It allows you to check the local and worldwide search volumes for specific keywords, in addition to lots of related keywords (absolute gold) and competitiveness of the keywords. It's a virtual goldmine resource for online entrepreneurs looking for profitable niches.

Any main keyword that has a search volume of more than 1000 global exact match searches per month is good to begin with. Some prefer picking keywords with over 2,000 exact match global searches, but 1,000 searches is decent enough. You want keywords which are fairly in demand without being exceedingly competitive.

For instance, let's take the keyword 'How to surf' on Google. It may give you close to 1,00,000 organic search results, which is fairly low competition. Again, check for the paid ads. If there are only a couple of them after refreshing the page multiple times, it may be a good to go niche.

It really depends upon your individual strategy. Some folks like dabbling in highly competitive niches where all the money is so even if they get a small slice of the pie, it's a lot of money. Others prefer dominating a little-known niche and earning a majority of the profits to be made from it.

Check if there are any PPC pay-per-click advertisers bidding for the keyword on Google Adwords. If there is a lot of frenzied activity and bidding for the keyword, it may be high competition. Sometimes, keywords have a large number of organic searches but few paid bidding. Based on whether you are opting for organic or paid searches, you might want to consider the two before moving ahead.

Let's consider another key phrase 'law of attraction'. A simple Google search throws up about a few million competing pages for the topic. It barely has any PPC ads though. This simply means that it will be challenging to rank on page 1 for the keyphrase (with a few million pages for competition) but you can consider PPC ads.

Look at Google's keyword suggestions offered by the Google Keyword Tool to understand this pattern. Are people looking for inexpensive eBooks or low priced/free information in the niche? What are readers typically looking for in the niche? Coaching programs? Courses?

Now check for an exact match search for 'Law of Attraction' course. The exact match search is lower than 50, which means it may be a challenge to work with this niche.

Next, use Google Trends for studying trends related to the niche you are contemplating. For instance, Law of Attractions show was at its peak in 2007 during the time Rhonda Byrne's *The Secret* popularized the theory. However, it shows a downward spiral ever since, which means you may not be able to build a very lucrative blog around it.

8. Identify Profitable Problems

No, this isn't about cashing in on other's misery but simply offering solutions that can better their life, while still making decent profits for your time and effort. Not all problems faced by people are similar. Some need a more aggressive sell, while others have customers just waiting to buy workable solutions.

Follow the pointers mentioned above for doing a basic keyword research for determining the number of monthly searches for a specific problem. Also, look at the number of long-tail keywords that suggest a desperate intent to seek a solution for the problem and the amount of high-quality information resources related to the problem available on the internet for free.

What are the kinds of solutions people are looking for within the niche? For instance, if its skin acne, are they looking for natural remedies, quick-fix skin supplements, creams or skin treatment advice? What is the typical language they are using on forums for expressing their problems? Use the same words and phrases to resonate with them. Include these in your sales or ad copy (more later) to make it more relevant and identifiable for your audience.

Chapter 4: Step by Step Guide for Creating an Affiliate Marketing Blog

Contrary to what shiny blogging courses will lead you to believe, setting up a profitable affiliate marketing blog isn't about throwing together a bunch of posts, adding a few affiliate offer links and sitting back to enjoy your profits.

A Blogging.com research recently revealed 81% of bloggers do not even reach a $100 benchmark. This hasn't got anything to do the limitations of blogging and everything to do with the blogger's mindset and attitude.

If you have a profitable niche, a workable traffic generation plan, a clever content strategy, valuable content and relevant affiliate offers, you increase your chances of creating a sustainable source of income with your affiliate blog.

So how do you go about creating a blog from scratch? The good news – you don't need any glossy, technical skills or programming know-how. It's easy to set up and have a blog running within a couple of hours. Here's a step-by-step guide.

1. Choose a Platform

Aspiring bloggers can begin with both self-hosted and free blogging platforms. However, bloggers who are serious about setting up a blog for making money should consider going with the self-hosted option. Free blogging platforms have several restrictions with regards to placing ads or earning revenue by promoting others' offers.

If your blog is a personal reflection diary or you are simply penning your thoughts down as a hobby, free blogging platforms may work. For more commercial purposes, self-hosted platforms can offer you far greater flexibility and control in managing your blog and revenue channels.

Free blogging platforms often have URLs that look like – blogname.blogspot.com or yourblogname.tumblr.com.

Self-hosted platforms such as WordPress.org can give you far more versatility and flexibility when it comes to the blog design, features and software plug-ins. You can have a unique domain name as opposed to a generic one offered by free platforms.

Opt for the WordPress.org self-hosted platform to build a more professional, beautiful and easy to navigate the blog.

2. Register a Domain Name

Your domain name becomes your brand identity. It should be a unique, memorable, catchy and identifiable name that reflects your blog's persona. Keep domain names easy to spell and free from special characters. It should immediately convey the essence of your blog in a few words.

Most affiliate marketers recommend going with a .com domain, although there's no reason not to opt for a .net or .org domain if the name you are looking for isn't available in the .com variation. However, .com has universal appeal and is synonymous with the internet. You can also opt for location specific domains if you are targeting people from a specific geographic location. There are several other domain extensions such. sports or .clubs or .travelling. Pick the one that best fits your blog's content and tone.

There is a perpetual debate about exact match domains versus brand-able domains. Exact match domains are domains which include your primary keyword such as

bestweightlosssupplements.com

Brandable domains, on the other hand, are catchier, more creative and memorable names such as crafthacks.com or problogger.com. You can opt to merge with the two (gadgetreviewexpert.com or travelbloggingauthority) or go with a clever brandable name since exact match domains don't necessarily earn you a top position in Google's search results.

Consider signing up for a Domain Privacy Protection option even if you skip all other domain name add-ons or additional offerings. It helps keep your personal contact information as a publisher from being visible on the public whois.net domain. In the absence of this add-on, anyone can access your details from the site.

3. Get a Hosting Service

There are literally hundreds of hosting service providers to choose from. Pick one that provides top grade customer service, offers good speed/performance and low downtime. An indiscriminate choice while selecting your hosting service can lead to several technical issues, which in turn can affect your blog's functionality and overall user experience. Go with reliable services that have established credentials and glowing reviews by well-known blog publishers.

Server reliability is an important criterion when it comes to selecting a hosting service. Opt for a host who operates on a solid server and reliable network of connections. The recommended or standard uptime score is 99.5% and more. Stay away from anything that's below 99%.

A shared hosting account is fine for supporting an optimized WordPress site with about 30,000 to 40,000 unique visitors/month. However, if you expect traffic to grow exponentially within the next couple of years, you will eventually want to opt for a dedicated server.

Opt for hosting services that allow you to add multiple domains.

Avoid jumping in with cheap sign-up offers. They will often end up costing a lot more during renewal. Read the terms and conditions carefully to ensure the hosting service renewal charges are acceptable to you or you'll simply end up hopping between hosts frequently. A decent hosting service will cost you $10 or below/month.

4. Install WordPress Blog

Once you receive a mail from your hosting service provider, you can activate your account by going to the control panel or cpanel section of the blog.

Simply click "Install WordPress" and you're good to go with the click of a single button.

You will receive your WordPress login and admin URL (www.blogname.com/wp-admin) information once the installation is completed.

You can go about changing the layout of the blog or selecting a different theme from the Appearances section.

WordPress utilizes multiple design templates popularly referred to as WordPress themes. It adds more visual appeal to your blog and makes it user-friendly. Themes can be installed and changed at the click of a button. WordPress has over 2,000 free and fully customizable themes, in addition to paid, premium themes created by platforms such as Themeforest.net.

Plugins are software channels that are installed to fulfill a particular function or feature within the blog. This can include everything from keeping your blog spam-free (Askimet plug-in) to improving the SEO score of the blog (Yoast plug-in).

Chapter 5: 13 Proven Tips for Improving Your Affiliate Conversions

So you have an amazing blog with a ton of high-quality content, arresting visuals and a neat layout. The affiliate ads/links are all in place and you've also started attracting a steady stream of visitors. Yet, conversion rates are low. People don't seem to check out your affiliate links, which is hampering the overall profitability of the blog.

To begin, don't expect profits overnight. You have to invest a few months in researching, studying and tweaking the system. Specific types of ads and links work better for some niches over others. It takes time to build traffic, get people excited about your products and eventually, get them to trust you enough to buy through your link.

You'll have to build your reputation and test different links. However, if you're witnessing disappointing low results for long, it may be time to change your strategy. Here are 10 proven strategies that are known to massively increase affiliate conversions (converting readers/audience into buyers)if implemented correctly.

1. Create a Sense of Urgency

This doesn't imply filling your blog with tons of "buy nows" and "take action today." It's all about creating a combination of logical and emotional copy to gradually build a sense of urgency to propel your audience into taking the desired action.

People may eventually want to take action and they may put it off for later and buy directly from the site), thus leading to you missing an affiliate sale. Therefore, creating a feeling of urgency is important to completing the action right away. The longer people take to make decisions, the tougher it is to convert them into buyers. Guide people into what you want them to do by stating it explicitly and making it easier for them.

Give them a reason to make that purchase decision right away. "Sign Up Now", "While Supplies Last", "Limited Period Offer", "Final Chance! Grab it While You Can!", "Don't Put This Off Any Further", "Buy One Get One Free – Expires Shortly" and other similar urgency creating a call to action copy. People are just waiting for a reason to pull that trigger. Give them the opportunity and you will significantly increase your affiliate conversions.

Create a feeling of paucity related to the product or service. Scarcity gets people into action mode. If you're offering unique bonuses, inform them that they are limited period and aren't being offered elsewhere.

Things like, "this special bonus is only available to the first 50 action takers" or "only 50 bonuses packs left" and other similar offers are great, especially during the launch phase of a product or service.

2. Flash Testimonials

Testimonials are big when it comes to establishing the credibility of a product or service. If done right, they can boost your conversions dramatically. Include social media or email screenshots when a product/service gets glowing reviews. Each time you receive a positive or encouraging feedback about the product/service, take permission and share it publically.

Request people for their pictures and include it with the testimonial to make it more personal and credible.

Prospective 'on the fence' buyers dig testimonials with pictures of real people like them who've loved the product or service. You can also check with your affiliate merchants. They may have a bank of testimonials you can use on your blog. If it's a high quality and reputed product, many people would've said positive things about it, which will only help in driving more sales.

3. Use Videos

This isn't a secret anymore and most affiliate marketers know the power of creating videos for marketing affiliate products/services. There are tons of videos you can create starting from How To's going right down to product demonstrations.

YouTube is the second most widely used search engine, and it's owned by the big G. Google ranks videos on YouTube favorably on its search results. You'll not just get a ton of organic traffic but also find a more receptive audience versus long, text-based content since videos are more personal and easy to follow.

Create a basic video with a regular phone camera to begin with, no flashy equipment needed really. If you prefer not being in front of the camera, create a Power Point Presentation or simply focus on the product. Sparkol and GoAnimate are worthy options for creating fun, easy to digest animated videos.

Videos not just increase your traffic but also increase your conversions significantly. Include links to the specific blog page related to the video at the end of the video.

4. Interlink

Many a times affiliate marketers complain about adding their links to several well-written blog posts and still getting disappointing results. How does one write blog posts that convert?

Write a single exhaustive and comprehensive tutorial and then keep linking other posts to it periodically.

One of the best strategies for increasing your affiliate profits is to create tutorials because you're actually showing them how to use a product rather than simply selling it to them or telling them they need it.

Product reviews, usability guides, resource lists, posts detailing before and after results, gift ideas and list based posts or round-ups can get you a ton of conversions. Create step-by-step guides that inform your audience about how to create something or use certain resources/tools. You can then include your suggestions as affiliate links within the blog.

For instance, if you create a step-by-step tutorial about setting up a WordPress blog, you can use your affiliate link for the hosting service provider or premium themes, while offering them valuable suggestions that can make their blog more effective. Show people how it's done or used rather than simply telling them to use it.

Don't just drop affiliate links everywhere. Create tutorials and link to other pages/post within the blog. Focus on driving people to the tutorial, so they are well-informed about the benefits of the product/service and how it's used. Your recommendations will earn more credibility.

You won't come across as a bird of prey waiting to catch unsuspecting victims if you take the trouble to offer more value to your audience with detailed tutorials.

5. Create a Resources Page/Section

One of the best tips for increasing your affiliate conversions without coming across as a seedy salesperson is to create a resources page for your blog.

You can list some of the best products and services that you've loved using and which you know will benefit your readers here. This is a great way to increase your credibility as an affiliate marketer rather than posting links everywhere. Direct people to your resource page for more information. You can also cite the resource page on your social media posts and Facebook groups without appearing spammy.

Referencing makes things easier for you and the readers – you don't feel guilty about simply selling to your readers without offering any real value.

6. Follow Ethical Practices

Nothing spells doom for affiliate marketers like resorting to unethical practices for making sales. Offering false or misleading information or directing people to products/services that are of little value to them is grossly dishonest.

People are sure to swear off buying from you once your reputation as a marketer is harmed. Avoid indulging in unethical, get rich quick practices if you are planning to build a long-term and sustainable source of passive income.

You owe a full disclosure to the audience ethically and legally. Inform them that the blog has affiliate links, and you get paid a small commission if they purchase through those links. Pitch it as a reward you earn you for investing your time and efforts in recommending the right products to your audience and running the information-rich blog resource for them.

This helps you come across as an honest and transparent marketer who offers value in exchange for commissions rather than a greedy person simply out to get their money. Also, make it a point to mention that they don't end up paying more for the product/service because you earn a commission on it. They will be paying the same prices as on the merchant's site. If there are any special promos or reduced price offers, mention them loud and clear.

7. Write Genuine Product Reviews

Create honest, detailed and easy to read reviews of the products or services you are promoting. Always be on the lookout for better ways to market your product without making it come across as a hard-sell.

Develop a personal and unique tone that connects with your audience. Share a personal story to add a more relatable or human element to your reviews.

Create balanced reviews that also include some flaws to help people make more informed choices. They will also appreciate a sincere effort to bring out both the good and bad of a product/service. Your audience will come to view you as a more authentic and credible source of information/reviews for the products or services you are promoting.

Use products personally before recommending them to your customers. It will award you a naturally well-informed tone. Focus on benefits rather than product features. Follow the WIIFM principle followed by top copywriters all across the world. WIIFM is simply What's In It For Me. Tell your audience what's in it for them instead of simply pitching features in a cut and dry staccato tone. Inform them about how the product can benefit them or why they really need it.

Create compelling, persuasive and pithy headlines to arouse the interest of your audience as 8 out of 10 readers make up their minds about whether to read a review or no based on your headline.

Make it a question-based headline that evokes a powerful emotional or tugs at their deepest fears or desires.

One of the biggest ways to enhance user experience and increase conversions is to share the pros and cons of a product in a bullet format after drafting a comprehensive review covering different aspects of it. You can rate the product/service on a scale of 1-10 on every aspect.

For instance, if you are reviewing a food processor, you can divide it into various sections such as usability/functionality, design, value for money etc. Then write detailed reviews for every aspect of the product. What can readers expect from the product in terms of usability or design? Furthermore, give it an overall rating on a scale of 1-10. At the end, sum up the review with the pros and cons of the product mentioned in a bullet point format.

Conclude with a single line that best describes the product, complete with its pros and cons.

8. Use A/B or Split Testing

Split testing is often used by affiliate marketers across the world for increasing their conversions. A/B or Split testing can be utilized for deciding what works best between two different versions of a headline, page layout, color, text, affiliate offers, navigation, the size of buttons, visuals and more.

You start by creating two distinctly different headlines or other factors to be tested. An A/B testing software channelizes half the traffic to page A and the other half to page B. Both pages feature a call to action. Ultimately, you can determine how many people from both pages took action to understand which headline or call or action works better than the other.

In the early stages of the business, have at least one A/B split test active on the blog at any point in time. Remember – there's no one size fits all strategy for affiliate marketing success. You'll know what works and doesn't work for you based on continuous testing. Remember to test only one aspect at a time to nail down what's working and what's not. If you end up split testing too many aspects, you won't be able to pin down the exact parameter working in favor of or against your conversion rate.

Also, test for the action button size and call to action copy. Certain call to action words work wonderfully for some niches. For instance, "Demo/Trial" works well for software products, while "checkout/purchase" is great for information reports, courses and eBooks.

9. Create a Clear and Persuasive Value Proposition

Value proposition is one of the most important factors for determining your conversion rate. How do you define a value proposition? It is what's in it for the customer? Why should he/she buy from you? How can the product benefit him/her or add value to his/her life?

If you could just describe the product or service you are promoting in 10 words, what would your pitch be?

Strengthen your value proposition by making the prospect of buying from you irresistible. It should be something that differentiates the product/service from competing products/services. It should be a unique benefit. Even if the product/service you are promoting matches the competitor's products/services on every parameter, it should stand out in one area.

Make this area where your product/service excels the unique value proposition while promoting the product. Creating a value proposition is the key factor for getting people to make purchase-related decisions. Keep fine-tuning your value proposition until you can summarize it with a single, credible sentence. Keep optimizing your value proposition with the help of split testing.

10. Set Up a Sales Funnel or Cycle

If you want people to buy from your affiliate link the moment they land up on your site, you're living in an illusionary world. Don't ask for the sales too fast. Follow a process which makes it almost impossible for the reader to refuse your offer.

One of the biggest blunders internet marketers make is to ask for a sign-up sale too quickly without investing time in building a trustful relationship. A majority of the time people are casually browsing for information and not in the psychological zone of buying. As an affiliate marketer, you have to gently transport them from the browsing zone to the buyer zone with consistent efforts and a well-planned sales funnel.

The costlier or complicated your chosen product/service is, the longer it will take for people to make a purchase decision. Give people time to commit. Slow down a bit in the beginning and focus on building trust, developing a rapport and demonstrating your expertise.

Let us say you're promoting a course on how to create a highly profitable travel blog. Your goal is to get as many aspiring travel bloggers and those seeking nomadic work lifestyle to sign up for your course.

Your visitors' goal is to learn more about the secrets of being a successful travel blogger. So what do you do to fulfill both these goals?

Start by offering free travel blogging advice though your blog, videos, information reports, tutorials, and infographics.

Win the trust of aspiring travel bloggers and become their "go-to" advisor for everything related to travel blogging.

Give them a strong reason to subscribe to your email list in the form of valuable information or resources (for example a list of travel niches within the vast general travel niche). You can also offer free drip content travel blogging video courses. This can include the basics.

Direct them to your sales copy and finally ask for that much wanted sale! Seasoned internet marketers believe that it takes a minimum of 7 contacts before a prospective customer feels comfortable to commit to a purchase from you. This isn't research backed, of course. However, it elucidates the point that the stronger your relationship with your audience, the likelier they are to purchase from you.

Not just that, they also become evangelists for your products/services. Slow down. Offer real value and trust before asking for a sale. This is why you must capture their mail using an opt-in service so you can keep the conversation going.

11. Avoid Jargon

Clarity overrides complicated sounding technical expertise all the way. Have you read something like, "Complete revenue-centric promotion automation and marketing effectiveness strategies unleash beneficial collaboration throughout the gross revenue cycle" only to wonder what the hell it means.

Can you fathom how tough you make it for your customers in a bid to impress them with heavy technical jargon?

Forget trying to woo your audience with fancy and complicated sounding technical jargon. Stick to expressing your ideas clearly and persuasively. Write for everyday people. Clarity is the one aspect that even seasoned internet markets struggle with.

One of the best strategies for making your content clear and more palpable for your audience is to re-phrase it as if you are talking about the service/product to your closest friend. If something doesn't sound like you would use it in a talk with your close buddies, re-phrase it.

12. Foresee and Kill Objections

Objections will almost always rear their head in the minds of customers when they read reviews or pitches about products/services you are trying to promote. There will be some obvious and subconscious objections that you will have to slay to get them to purchase through your affiliate link.

When you pre-determine these concerns and tackle them in your copy, you increase your chances of converting a reader into a buyer. Addressing the prospective buyer's objections in your sales copy eliminates their apprehensions and propels them to take faster action in the desired direction. Tackle all possible issues that prevent them from buying.

Create a comprehensive list of all potential hesitations, objections, and concerns prospective customers can come up with. Add as much in your sales copy to handle these objections.

For instance: An objection that can arise in a reader's mind is "You really don't understand the problem I am facing. Kill this by explaining about how the product or service can solve that their problem.

What if the product or service doesn't work as expected for me? Include a few testimonials of people who've benefited hugely from the product or service. They can be from different sections or groups to add more variety to the audience base.

There are cheaper alternatives for the product/service. This is the classic price versus value syndrome. Inform customers what it's going to cost them to not buy your product over focusing on its price. It's the value that counts at the end of the day.

Compare the product or service you're promoting with competing products. Justify your price versus the competitor prices. Compare the benefits with the benefits offered by competitors to show them the value of buying from you. Prove the real value of the products or services you are promoting. Seek inputs from your social circle as a test audience to determine every possible objection and come up with a resounding copy that puts it to rest.

13. Include Affiliate Links within Blog Posts

You can occasionally embed affiliate links within blog posts. This isn't to say that you write specific blog posts with the sole intention of promoting a product to your audience. However, if you think a particular product or service fits well within a post and can help your blog audience, by all means, promote it within the post. Just ensure you use this tactic sparingly and not litter every post with tons of links that annoy your readers.

If you've used the product/service and are happy with its results, you can go ahead and confidently recommend it to your readers. People are smart and will be able to tell when you've written a post specifically for pedaling a bunch of offers and when you offer valuable and helpful recommendations based on your experience.

Chapter 6: How to Pick Profitable Affiliate Offers

Affiliate marketing is a huge and thriving online money making industry, helping thousands of professional bloggers and marketers reap rich profits from it. With more big players getting involved, there are even bigger opportunities for upcoming and veteran bloggers alike to make cool profits with their blogs.

With a large variety of enterprises now realizing the ingenuity of the affiliate model, most affiliate marketers are a part of affiliate marketing networks or affiliate marketplace that allows you to access and sign up for several offers from a single platform.

Some popular affiliate marketing networks are ClickBank, SharASale, OfferVault, CJ Affiliate, MarketHealth, Amazon Associates, MarketLeverage, PepperJam Network and Rakuten LinkShare.

Finding the Right ClickBank Products

ClickBank is one of the largest and most reputed platforms for digital products in virtually every conceivable category. The commissions for digital products can be reasonably high because the merchant does not incur raw material or shipping/handling costs.

All users need to do to access the product is to click on a link to download it. This makes the prospect of selling digital products extremely lucrative. Though you may need to sell a high volume of it to make decent profits, digital products also find fast buyers since they are considerably inexpensive and help solve major problems for a specific audience.

Here are some expert pointers for picking the right ClickBank products to promote.

1. Commission Percentage

Filter products according to their commission percentage. Any product that has a commission percentage of less than 60% may be a time-waster. A majority of ClickBank's products are sold for $30-80. This means you should be able to garner at least $18-20 per sale on an average. There are several affiliate products with a neat commission rate of 60% and more. Some offers even go as much as 75%. These are your winners.

However with rules come exceptions too. There are some high ticket items that offer a 50% commission rate, which may be worth considering too. Since these are high priced items, even a 50% payout works out to be lucrative. As a rule of thumb, don't opt for any product that goes below 50% in its commission payout when it's a non-subscription based product. It may just not be worth the time and effort you invest to promote the program.

Another exception is subscription based or recurring bill items, where affiliate marketers earn commissions every time buyers renew their membership or subscription. This is working once to gain a buyer, and earning commission multiple times for the single sale. In such a scenario, you can go with a 40% payout or below because you are earning profits several times for the sale.

2. Gravity Rating

Gravity rating is another important criterion to be considered while picking profitable ClickBank products. Avoid being flustered by complicated terminology. Gravity rating is nothing but a rank assigned to ClickBank digital products based on their sales figures garnered by various affiliate promoters.

High gravity rating items are simply those products that have performed well or are in demand, and several marketers are making money by promoting it. Though gravity rating is an important consideration while picking your product, you can also promote new products with low gravity.

A high gravity (100+) indicates high competition, with a lot of players involved in selling the product or service. However, competition also reflects that there's abundant demand for products within the niche. So competition isn't always a bad thing. It means there's a lot of potential for partnerships and collaborations with other marketers.

 If you spot a new yet promising and high-quality product that can of benefit for the audience, consider it. There may be far less competition than popular products and you may end up bagging a fair share of the profit pie before other marketers discover it.

3. Look at the Sales Page

One of the most infallible techniques for picking the right ClickBank products is to thoroughly assess its sales page. You will instantly realize the potential of the product by scanning through its marketing copy.

Lengthy, persuasively drafted, detailed and genuine sales copy can dramatically increase your conversions. People relate to a honestly written copy that appeals to their logical and emotional side.

Compare the sales copy of the product you are planning to promote with its closest competitor. Does your affiliate merchant have a more persuasive pitch? Does it appeal to your target audience? Does the product you are contemplating promoting have something that others don't and does the sales copy convey this convincingly? Is the sales page more visually attractive than the competitors? If you were a customer, would you be tempted to buy the product right away after reading the copy?

Look at factors such as credibility of the merchant, his/her expertise in the subject, the quality of the content and the value it will add to your reader's life. It is fairly easy to tell apart high-quality products from the turkeys.

Another tip is to go to Alexa.com and measure the amount of traffic received by the main offer URL or the sales page. This will give you a good idea if it's an old or new offer. Of course, being new doesn't necessarily mean you should disqualify it. However, it helps to promote offers that are time tested and have been around for a while. New offers may require a more creative approach since you may not have resources such as testimonials, reviews etc. to promote it.

However by and large, if it's a high-quality product (created by a credible merchant) that offers a solid value proposition to your target audience, got for it.

Finding The Right CPA Programs

CPA or Cost-Per-Acquisition offers can help you make a quick profits since they do not require the user to buy anything. All the readers need to do is enter some information for a free trial or for companies to contact them and you end up earning a commission each time they enter their details.

Some companies offer free trials for skin or weight loss supplements. They need the customer's zip code to send them their free trial bottles. Other times, insurance companies may look for leads for offering free quotes. They may need your reader's contact details to communicate with them about their requirements.

Some popular affiliate marketplaces for CPA programs are NeverBlue, MarketHealth, and PeerFly.

Here are some winning pointers on picking the right CPA offers.

1. Opt for CPA offers that help you make at least $1 per acquisition. There are lots of programs out there offering commission rates of $0.20 and lower. These may not be worth it unless your site boasts of heavy traffic and sign-ups.

2. Try and hunt for profitable zip code offers in your niche. Not all niches will have them of course. They are more prevalent with niches related to real estate, finance, insurance, loans etc. However, zip code programs can be one of the best at converting. All users need to do is enter a valid zip code for you to earn a commission.

Email submissions might be trickier to convert but may offer higher commission. The affiliate merchant may be trying to build an email list and will pay you each time a user submits a valid email address.

If you have a focused niche and fairly high traffic, you can get a ton of exclusive offers from individual advertisers looking to set-up high paying programs on your blog.

For instance, if you run a blog about vacationing in Antigua, local vacation rental companies may come up with special offers to pay you a nice commission each time a prospective Antigua vacationer signs up with an email or other contact details for the company to get in touch with them.

3. Go carefully through the offer restrictions. Many CPA offers look awesome on the face of it and get marketers all excited only for them to realize that they come with a bunch of unflattering terms and conditions.

Some programs can only be promoted through email, while others cannot be promoted on a certain medium. You really want to be able to promote your offers freely without a ton of clauses. Carefully go through the T & C of each offer before you consider promoting it.

For some offers, it is alright to offer incentives to your readers for signing up, which is basically bribing them to get their details. Others strictly prohibit this practice and instantly ban marketers doing it from their network. You have to know what is permitted and prohibited within the offer to prevent getting into trouble.

4. Talk to your affiliate manager. Most people are intimidated by the prospect of talking to their affiliate manager and hence leave a lot of money on the table for their competitors by missing out on cool insider tips.

Get in touch with your affiliate manager with a list of specific and not generic questions. For instance, if you notice that a majority of your traffic comes from social networking platforms, ask for offers that convert well on social media. Get information such as the type of landing pages that work well for the social media audience or headlines you can use to appeal to Facebook, Twitter, and Instagram users.

Establish a good rapport with your affiliate manager to gather those all important pointers and suggestions. Send greetings on holidays and special occasions. Appreciate the help they extend to you by sending a simple Thank You card. They will be glad to go out of the way to help you when you appreciate their efforts.

5. Keep an eye on fresh offers. Being one of the first promoters to try an offer gives you the early entrant advantage. Try new, relevant CPA offers at least once before forming an opinion about them.

One of the biggest advantages of trying fresh affiliate offers is there's virtually no competition involved. You are basically taking home a route which is empty and comfortable over another which is jammed with vehicles.

The offer isn't proven to be a winner yet, but it's new and there's no competition so there's really no harm in trying it. Who knows? You may be able to make it a high seller or winner with your ingenious promotion skills.

Sometimes, affiliate networks have offers that haven't made it to the public domain yet. They may run internal tests before publically releasing it or they may only allow a handful of marketers to promote that offer. Try and be in the initial batch of promoters for new offers instead of jumping on the bandwagon once the program is saturated.

6. Check out AffPaying.com. Copy-paste the affiliate network's name into AffPaying review's search option. Click the magnifying glass icon. Once the network you are keen on joining appears, click on it. You have details such as payment frequency, payment methods, referral earning system and much more about the network at your fingertips.

Watch out for the network's rating distribution. If there are several 5 and 4-stars and few 1 and 2-stars, this may very well be a legitimate network. On the other hand, a network page that has tons of low 1 and 2-stars ratings may not be worth signing up for. Join networks that have favorable ratings. Once approved, start promoting their offer on your blog immediately.

7. If you're really serious about your affiliate marketing business and want to up the game, consider being a part of large affiliate marketing conferences/networking events such as the annual Affiliate Summit. You'll meet experienced and newbie affiliate marketers, and learn a ton about killer affiliate marketing offers, and trends within the industry in general.

Top Strategies for Picking Winning Affiliate Products

Stalk Competitors

Okay, not literally but you get the point right? Create a list of 10-20 most popular websites/blogs within your niche. Find out what affiliate offers they are involved in promoting. Analyze their tactics to know how they are broadening their audience reach. Answer these questions for best results.

What is the total number of products/services they are promoting?

What type of content are they creating - reviews, product comparison tables and/or video testimonials?

What are the strategies they use for building their email list?

How often do they update their website or blog?

What social media promotion strategies do they use to drive users to their blog? In what way does it add to their conversion rate?

Sales Tracking Systems

The efficiency of the affiliate referral tracking system is integral to building a solid affiliate marketing business. Ensure there aren't any loopholes in the process. Ascertain that all the links are properly set-up so you're doing everything right from your end.

Opt to work only with vendors who have a fool-proof affiliate link tracking system. You don't want to spend a ton of time, money and effort promoting offers for which you aren't credited due to a fault in their system.

Check whether each link on your site leads to the destination link and if the destination link has your unique affiliate code. If you are permitted to buy from your link, do that to verify if you are being credited for sales made through your affiliate link. Lastly, ensure that you are also included as an affiliate for the up-sells offered by the merchant post the original sale. This can add to your commission considerably.

Chapter 7: Fool-Proof Ways for Promoting Affiliate Offers

By now, you have a good understanding of what affiliate marketing is, how to improve your conversion rates, how to set up a professional-looking affiliate marketing blog, how to pick winning affiliate products, how to reduce your chances of failing at affiliate marketing and more. Some people do everything from using high ranking keywords to high-quality content creation to submitting articles all over the place and still do not witness the desired results.

Let's now look at using effective strategies for promoting your affiliate offers to your target audience.

1. Create a separate doorway entry page for every affiliate program you promote and market it on all relevant channels. Link a page within your blog to the doorway page. It is even more effective if you can grab a domain name for each individual page.

2. Ensure you submit the site to every available search engine. Several affiliate marketers overlook this basic step and leave out a ton of traffic in the bargain.

3. Create an eBook based on the products or services you are promoting and market it or submit it to various eBook sites. You can promote good offers through the eBook. Just keep it limited to a few good offers and don't go overboard with the affiliate links.

4. Email marketing is another great tool for promoting your products and services to a highly targeted audience. Write a killer promotional mail and use a service like MailChimp to send it to 2,000 email recipients free every month.

5. Run a Google Adwords campaign. Visual ads and video ads work wonderfully for promoting affiliate marketing offers.

6. Join as many online forums within your niche as possible. Include a link back to your blog in your profile signature section. Try and leave behind well-researched, detailed and informative comments on relevant forums to establish your authority and get people curious about your blog.

7. Offer free and well-written reports (check out easyplr.com for professionally written reports on several topics) in exchange for an email address. Send monthly newsletters to your mail list and promote the month's most buzz-worthy offers through them. You can also do a product giveaway to get tons of sign-up leads from casual browsers.

8. Outreach. Get in touch with influencers from your niche or do round-ups featuring several influencers from the niche. They will most likely share these round-ups among their several thousand social media followers. You can include a few powerful offers on these round-up pages. For instance, you can get in touch with beauty bloggers and ask them for their number one anti-aging tip. They love to be pitched as experts and will share the link on their social media pages for skincare, make-up and beauty enthusiasts.

14. Guest blogging is another wonderful way to drive traffic to your blog posts. Network with other influencers within your niche. Propose creating a detailed and informative post for their audience. You can collaborate on supplementary blogs. For instance, if there's a popular wedding related blog and your

blog is dedicated to fashion, you can propose to write a "top wedding gown trends for 2017" post for their blog.

Include links to your blog in the author bio. If people love reading your post (and they'll be lots of readers if you pick a busy blog), they will usually check out your blog. The aim is to establish yourself as a go-to authority in your niche.

15. Once you earn some profits, you can think about scaling it up with Google or Facebook advertising. You can also use PPC ads for getting people to sign-up for a webinar, grow your email list or simply get more end sales.

16. Unlock the potential of software tools that make the process of promoting your offers on your blog easier for you and more palpable for your audience. A tool such Skimlinks can instantly change existing product and business links within your posts into affiliate links to help save time and effort. It also picks up product recommendations or references and converts it into links for readers to buy from, thus helping you monetize your blog posts.

Promoting Affiliate Offers on Social Media

1. Get your social media users/followers to interact before driving them to your blog. Social media that receive plenty of user activity such as likes, shares, comments etc. are a sign of strong social signal (or social proof). It means your social media accounts receive plenty of traction, which is a good sign when it comes to determining the organic ranking on pages by search engines.

Urge readers to like, comment or share posts to increase the activity on your pages. Ensure that you reply to individual comments left by readers to build lasting relationships. This broadens your reach as well as gives you a lot of repeat purchases from existing customers. People buy from other people who care about them and not faceless bots.

Social media users like being told what action you want them to perform. For instance, if you post the picture of a cute kitten, people will react in the form of likes, shares, and comments. Now try posting the same visual, with a "Click Like or Share if you Want to Snuggle up With This Cute Kitty!" I can put all my money you will garner more "likes" or "shares" by including that phrase alone.

Something like, if you like puppies click like, if you adore kitties share and if you're a fan of both, comment works even if it sounds cheesy. You could also ask for suggestions. Help us name this cute kitty. These are audience interaction baits. You just need to put a well-thought and creative bait out there for your audience to grab.

2. Don't sell all the time. The rule should be 80:20, where 80% of the time you are only engaging, entertaining or informing your audience to sell effectively 20% of the time. Most people are on social networks for fun and entertainment. Don't try to pitch your offers on every post. Include links only sparingly, wherever appropriate.

Use the social media to gain attention, trust, loyalty and a reputation rather than hard-selling affiliate offers.

The thumb rule of not simply plugging products but informing your audience why it is useful for them is even truer for the social media. Social media users don't take too kindly to feeds overloaded with sales pitches. They like useful, informative and entertaining posts that can be shared, enjoyed or benefitted from by everyone. Create such posts of what they find high value in, include your affiliate links and share links to the post on your social media pages. Keep the tone genuine and help your followers make informed choices if you really want to ace the affiliate marketing game on social networks.

3. Use graphics generously. Do we prefer reading periodicals with images/visuals or simple endless text paragraphs? Your readers are no different. Use lots of attractive images on your Facebook and Instagram pages while promoting your affiliate offer. Use gifs, memes, videos and infographics (Use a tool like Canva) for adding a dash of humor or discussion points to your posts making them more shareable. Use a combination of entertaining and informative imagery, and you'll keep your followers hooked.

4. Add affiliate links to Pinterest posts. Pinterest recently lifted restrictions in adding affiliate links within pins, thus opening a whole new world for affiliate marketers to promote their products/services using stunning visuals.

Create a brandable board that reflects your business/blog persona. Keep all images on the board consistent with this persona. Pinterest users should be able to tell what your blog is all about without digging too much. Remember in the online world, every time you make people take extra effort, you're taking them away from completing the desired action. Use keywords in your pin board titles. Populate every board with pins you know your followers will be interested in.

Find images for products or services you want to promote and pin it to a relevant board you've created. For instance, if you're selling a product related to men's grooming, you may want to pin it to the father's day gifts board you've created.

Next, go to the 'edit this pin' option and delete the original web URL in the website box and add your unique affiliate link. Click save and you're done. Promote your pins on other social networks or use the paid promoted pins option for promoting specific pins with live affiliate links.

5. Compliment industry influencers. You can leverage a lot from the following of the industry's biggest players. Simply create a post featuring them as experts and they'll be more than happy to share it with their fans/followers. For instance, if you run a food related blog, you can create a "Top 10 Food Bloggers who've Inspired My Journey" or "10 Most Successful Food Bloggers for the Year." Send a message to the all featured bloggers along with a link to the piece. The influencers will almost always share the link with their followers.

Doing this regularly can earn your affiliate blog thousands of visitors every month while building you a considerable following and high conversions.

6. Refer followers to your resources page. If sharing an affiliate link on social media networks appears too salesy and bold, direct followers who may be interested in more information to a separate Resources Page, where you can promote hand-picked offers that you've personally used and benefitted from. Something like "Here are the blog building tools I've used to create my travel blog."

You can then go on to promote the host provider, themes, and other tools. Another tip will be to create a resource list like "top 10 must have resources for creating a stunning travel blog." Here you can promote the best tools for creating a travel blog from auto responders to stock image services – the list is endless. Some people with groups specifically ask for guidance or resource recommendations. Use the opportunity to drive people to your post.

7. Create special interest groups and communities rather than business pages. For instance, if you run a blog about training puppies, you can create a group or community for dog lovers or pet owners. People can discuss their pet related issues and experiences by engaging in a continuous dialogue. You can

offer lots of helpful suggestions and solutions to other dog lovers. This is great for fostering a community feeling or feeling of belongingness before people buy from you.

8. Use aggregator sites such as Quora or Reddit for promoting relevant posts. However, exercise caution when it comes to promoting your blog on these sites. Don't spam them to for worthless backlinks. Link to a post only when it directly answers the question or offers suggestions about questions posted by users. You can get a targeted traffic of users who are already looking for a specific solution offered by you. They are desperately seeking solutions, and may well buy into your proposition.

9. Use free tools such as Hootsuite for posting links to your newest post across several social media sites with a few clicks. Schedule posts before time to make the process more time-saving and efficient.

10. Run a live Facebook training for promoting your affiliate offers. Here's how you can go about doing it. Firstly, choose a single product or service that you want to recommend to your audience during the broadcast. Again, it should be related to the training and something that will offer them value.

Formulate a training script around the product or service you are promoting. For instance, if you are promoting a social media marketing course, structure a training topic such as how to gain the first 10,000 followers on Twitter or Facebook. Keep the outline restricted to 3-5 main points. Use a tool such as PrettyLink for cloaking your link to make it appear more attractive. Shortened and cloaked links appear less spammy and more credible recommendations to the audience.

Put as much of your personality into the training as possible to make it unique and interesting. Add generous doses of wit, humor, trivia and statistics. Once the live broadcast concludes, edit your video status and include the link. You now have a training session that can be permanently referred along with your affiliate link.

One way to encourage people to purchase through your link is to sweeten the deal by adding a bonus. It could be a physical item or digital product or informational report or complimentary shipping, access to a private membership group, a coupon code or a free training session. Fence-sitters respond brilliantly to incentives. Create a deadline on the incentives for even greater impact. It will create a sense of urgency, and lead people to purchase the product/service through your link right away.

11. Create an Instagram shop. There's a ton of money to be made on Instagram if you do it right. The platform doesn't permit the use of links within posts, though you can include a link to your bio or profile. A majority of bloggers will include a link to their blog or a squeeze page. However, if you are a really smart affiliate marketer (which I have no doubt about), you will use this sole link for a more resourceful purpose.

Yes, you nailed it. An Instagram shop! Create a unique, shop-style page, and direct users to it from you're the link in your bio. Check if your affiliate program permits you to use links on Instagram images before using this strategy.

To begin with, add an attractive looking link (PrettyLink to the rescue again) in your bio. Each time you add an image to the shop, refer to the profile or bio link. Every time you suggest a product or service, make sure to add an affiliate link. Visitors will be able to view a whole lot of your products all at once on the shop and click on images. If you've included your unique affiliate link, they'll automatically be redirected to the product page for their purchase.

Promoting Affiliate Offers With Paid Facebook Ads

Facebook ads have a huge advantage over many other paid advertising offers when it comes to promoting affiliate products or services. It gives the marketer access to a large pool of laser targeted audiences based on everything from their hobbies to the magazines they read to the food they like. You can target people based on their recent life events, their professions, hell even where they've recently traveled. That's a goldmine for affiliates who know how to harness the power of Facebook advertising.

Here are a few tips expert tips for marketing affiliate offers using Facebook's paid ad option.

1. Be super specific when it comes to selecting your audience based on their gender, age range, geographic location, interests and other demographics. You'll ensure a better response to your ads if you keep them focused. Keeping it more generic may not earn your ad the desired clicks, and even if they do – the conversion rates will be low. Don't burn your money by opting for a larger albeit unfocused audience.

2. Use the power of slideshows, graphics, infographics and videos in your ads to convey your message more persuasively. Split test your ads using a maximum of 6 different visuals to know which works best. Facebook advertising is a brilliant tool for spilled testing what works with your audience and what doesn't. The perfect image size for an FB ad is 1200 x 628 in a .png format.

Use bright, colorful and high-resolution images for greater appeal. Even a simple tip like editing your images using an app like Fotor can dramatically improve your ad conversion rate. Avoid unclear and dim pictures.

3. Headlines are the skeleton of your ad. Enter a powerful headline that directly addresses the concerns or interests of your target audience and echoes with them. The headline should be under 10-15 words, and ad body copy should be less than 90 symbols. Write an equally compelling Call-To-Action to drive readers into taking the desired action.

Keep your headlines gripping by posing questions related to the concerns or interests of your target audience.

Including statics is a powerful way of grabbing their attention. "Are you one of the 89% who suffers from stress related sleep disorders? Get Help!"

Make it a logical and emotional appeal. The problem-solution approach is one of the most fool-proof approaches. Present a problem or ask users if a problem exists in their life. Present your page/blog as a tool that seeks to offer them a solution for their problem. Urge them to take action if they want to eliminate the issue. The golden rule, remember? Tell them what's in it for them.

"Tired of searching for the perfect waffle maker? We've reviewed more than 50 models. Get yours today." Direct them to your review based blog post which contains affiliate links.

3. During the course of creating your ad, Facebook will offer you a choice of putting your ad on the desktop newsfeed, mobile feed or sidebar. Choose a single option because multiple feeds will end up confusing your testing plans. Mobile news feed is a good option to begin with. However, ensure you have a fully optimized blog if you are directing users to your blog.

4. Aim for at least 1% click through rate or CTR (CTR is the total number of clicks your advertisement receives divided by the total number of times it is displayed: clicks/impressions

=CTR) for your ads. If it's anything more than that, your ads are performing well. It simply means the layout, text, and appearance have struck a chord with your audience.

If your click through rate is anywhere below 1%, you can do with a little tweaking. Keep testing various versions of an ad until you discover your winning ads. Keep a close eye on the statistics. Measure the amount of clicks you gather and the cost per click for multiple ads. These insights are invaluable for creating profitable ads in future.

5. Assign a daily budget for your ads to avoid overspending. Start with $5-20 while you're testing. Once you've identified your winners, scale it up with a bigger budget.

6. This may not qualify as a paid advertising tip. However, a little-known way to garner more likes/fans for your page is to enable your "Similar Page Suggestions" option. Each time a user likes a competitor or similar page, Facebook offers similar page suggestions, which can get you some free likes. Go to your settings page and check "Similar Page Suggestions."

How to Come up with Blog Topics People Love to Share?

Creating epic content that gathers plenty of likes, comments and shares is the foundation of gaining traffic from social media. Detailed, entertaining and compellingly drafted content can generate a crazy amount of blog activity and social signals, which in turn can result in several affiliate sales. So how do you populate your blog with posts everyone loves? Here's the deal.

1. Keep a note based application such as Evernote handy. You'll get a ton of inspiration for blog topics while rummaging through your social media feed or even sitting in a café. Often, great ideas dawn upon us only to fade later. Ensure that you

make a note of your ideas before they vanish from your consciousness.

2. Go to a site like Buzzsumo and enter your topic in the search bar. You'll find a list of the most shared topics within the niche. You can then simply go on to create your own blog post and make it even better than the original post by adding something that it's missing. Include affiliate links within posts that have the potential to be hugely popular or viral.

3. Use tools such as keywordtool.io and enter your primary keyword. Look for topic ideas here and not search volume. For example, you may enter "Hawaii vacation guide" you'll find a string of related keywords such as "Hawaii travel tips" or "Hawaii vacation scams" or "Hawaii vacation rentals" and more. Pick up on these clues to create your affiliate blog posts. This is the information people are actually searching for and can benefit from.

You can create topics such as "Top 10 Hawaiian Vacation Packages", "10 Best Travel Tips for Couples Planning a Vacation to Hawaii", "How to Find Affordable Hawaii Travel Packages" and other similar topics.

You'll also discover a ton of hidden topics using Google's auto-complete feature. Create posts that offer value. If you are selling travel related merchandise like camping gear or travel bags, create a post like "10 Incredible Packing Tips While Going Camping."

4. Entering a few hashtags such as #hawaiivacation or #travelhawaii on social media searches is a great way for unearthing hot and trending topics related to the niche. Look at sources such as Pinterest for inspiration.

Look for topics that are explored from a unique or unusual angle. For example, every travel site does topics such as "Top 10 Tourist Attractions in Hawaii", how about doing a little snooping around and coming up with a topic like, "Did you know about Hawaii's Underground Bar Scene?" Look for different and off-beat stuff to make your posts more shareable.

You can also find plenty of topic ideas on Yahoo Answers, Hubspot, Reddit, and Quora. You'll know the kind of questions that are being raised in your niche and the solutions you can offer for those concerns in your blog post. For instance, you may discover people are looking around for the most useful apps for vacationers in Hawaii. You can then come up with a list of the best apps for Hawaii vacationers.

Chapter 8: List Building Secrets Marketers Don't Want You to Know

You're doing it all wrong if you aren't building a list at the outset. Bitter as it sounds - you are going to regret it later.

Your list is your gold mine. Internet marketers aren't exaggerating when they state, "the money is in the list." List building gives the opportunity to engage in constant conversation with a targeted and interested group of audience. Your list is something you truly own and can wield control over.

Google can come up with their next update and take away all your organic traffic almost overnight. It has happened to several marketers. The following that you've earned on the social media isn't owned by you. It is owned by a social media network, which can again change their policy and shut your shop before you can say Twitter. You are at best hiring the services of social media sites for building an audience.

In such a volatile, fickle and dynamic online scenario, your list is a database owned by you. Hence never overlook the power of building a list or using email marketing along with other forms of promotion for creating a loyal following.

Cheesy as it sounds, email marketing has the power to make you money on autopilot literally while you sleep. Once you have a list of targeted customers interested in the products or services you are promoting, you can pitch a ton of useful offers. You can promote anything from digital products to physical products to courses/membership sites as an affiliate.

You can send exclusive offer flyers, monthly newsletters, new product promos, launch offers, free eBooks and just about anything to your audience once you have their email.

So, how does one build that golden list? Here's how

1. Use a reputed and dedicated email marketing service provider like MailChimp or Aweber. They offer a full solution for all your email marketing needs, including automating new sign-ups, shooting emails and presenting statistics. Depending on your usage, you can opt for a fixed monthly subscription fee or fee-based on the volume of sent emails.

2. Give away tremendously useful or valuable lead magnets and free information. This should be a piece of information, report or checklist that isn't easily available on the internet. This should be the result of deep research, expert information or something that few people have knowledge of.

For instance, if you have a blog about weddings, you can have a list of "top 50 budget friendly destination wedding hotspots for 2017" or "the ultimate wedding planning checklist" or "10 wedding speech ideas." People love ideas, suggestions, and lists that cut down their research efforts.

Similarly, if your blog is about making money online, you can create a report about the niches or type of content that wows social media audiences or headline/email templates that they can use for reaching out to their customers.

Give out little-known secrets people don't generally share if you want your readers to part with their email in exchange. Grab the attention of your audience by offering them a value proposition that's impossible to refuse.

3. Ask for minimal information with your opt-in form. The longer it takes for people to enter their details, the higher are

the chances of them simply abandoning the process. Ask only for their email or email and name if you want to make your emails more personal. Don't ask for any more details if you want better conversions rates. Opt-in forms can be included within your blog by pasting an uncomplicated code provided by the email marketing service provider.

4. Leverage other people's lists too to create your own. If there's a complementary blog whose mail list can benefit from the products/services promoted by you, approach the blog owner for creating posts for their monthly newsletter.

You can also plug a post on another newsletter in exchange for offering the blog owner/marketer a specialized service. Think about drafting or editing a press release or creating a bunch of social media posts. They will be glad to mention you in their newsletter or offer you a post on it if they can get something valuable in return.

Plenty of internet and affiliate marketers suffer from the "it's a dog eat dog world out here" syndrome. Learn to collaborate rather than compete. Leverage the power of other people's skills and audience for forming mutually beneficial partners. This way, you won't just survive but conquer the world of affiliate marketing. Always be on the lookout for collaboration opportunities. Broaden your audience base by dipping into other people's user base.

5. Create a special social media contest, promo or giveaway. To be eligible for the contest or giveaway, users have to share their email. If you have a considerable social media following, it's a good opportunity to turn them into mail subscribers.

Give informative digital products or physical products related to your blog topic. The goal is to sign up folks who will truly be interested in your affiliate promotions. Don't overdo this tactic though or you'll get a ton of worthless sign-ups only after the rewards.

6. One of the biggest mistakes affiliate marketers make with their list is that they attempt to sell with each mail. Much of the goal of this list is to get people on your list to buy from you, selling with every mail sounds like a terribly selfish pursuit. It is bound to result in heavy unsubscribing, further plunging your profits.

Focus on offering free information every once in a while to retain folks on your list. Give them a reason to stay back by including free value over hard sell. Free information can also include pre-selling mails. Occasionally, you can subscribe them with freebies such as an eBook or some free tools/subscriptions that can really help them. It is a great way to thank them for being on your list.

As a rule, reserve two-thirds of your emails for free information (newsletters, free reports etc.) and one-third for aggressive sales.

7. Add an opt-in form to your blog's About Us page. About pages have one of the best opt-in rates on the blog. When people click to learn more about your blog, they are generally interested in knowing more about you. Once they're convinced they can benefit from the blog, they're ready to sign-up immediately. If you don't include an opt-in form within the top paragraphs of the About Us page, it's a huge missed opportunity.

8. Cover new verticals. Don't keep yourself restricted to a single segment or vertical when it comes to list building. For instance, if you are blog publisher for a blog on making money online, you can target writers, photographers, craft enthusiasts, stay at home moms and other groups who may be interested in

making money online from their skills. Create a different list for each vertical to allow you to target each segment of your audience with relevant offers.

Repurpose your available content to suit different markets. You've already dug the foundation for your primary market. All you're doing now is adding new levels or floors to the structure. You can always play around with the specifics when you a have a general skeleton in place.

9. Play by the book if you want long-term success. Adhere to the terms and conditions of specific programs if you want to make it a profitable source of income without getting into trouble. Also, comply with all email marketing laws, prominently the CAN-SPAM Act. Read FTC guides or other regulatory body rules prevalent in the region you're operating in.

Don't try to circumvent laws or try to beat the system with black hat tricks. You may gloat about your success in the initial stages before the unethical practices catch up with you. Understand laws related to internet, affiliate, and email marketing to avoid landing in hot soup.

Chapter 9: Search Engine Optimizing Your Affiliate Marketing Posts

Search engines are still one of the biggest sources of organic traffic. You have an audience that is actively seeking the solution you are promoting. Users are searching for products, services, and solutions related to your niche with specific keywords.

When you include these keywords and other optimization factors in your posts, you boost your chances of ranking high for relevant keywords on search engine results. You need to feature on the first couple of pages on Google's search to gain considerable organic traffic.

Here are a few proven tips for optimizing your blog posts to increase your organic reach through search engines.

1. Make is a practice to utilize H1, H2 and H3 HTML header tags. Include a title tag or the page by including about 2-3 related keywords. Also, always include a meta title (the title of the page displayed on search result pages and not the actual post title) and meta description (again, the description for the page as displayed in search engine results). The meta title and meta description should be below 60 and 160 characters respectively. This makes it easy for search engine bots to locate your content among other pages.

2. Integrate keywords naturally and seamlessly into your blog posts. Don't make them appear forced and irrelevant. Stuffing your blog posts with popular keywords just to increase your placement rank will, in turn, earn you a lifetime ban by Google.

Few things irk Google more than low quality, such as affiliate farm blogs designed only to sell a bunch of spammy affiliate products/services.

3. Use the useful Alt tag for all images. Include relevant, clear and appropriate keywords that back the text content. This makes it easier for your post to be located through a Google Image search.

4. Using long tail keywords is always a good strategy. You target a very specific need or a group of buyers who are already half way through the buying cycle. Instead of "acne remedies", you can include more fleshed out keywords such as, "how to get rid of face acne using natural remedies." See what we did there? More focused keywords for a higher rank and lesser competition.

5. Interlink to other posts within your blog. This will decrease your site's bounce rate and will keep people on your site for longer (one of the important algorithms for ranking your page on search engines). It also enhances the overall user experience and makes it easy for people to access a bunch of related posts.

6. Search engines dig posts that are fresh, regularly updated and detailed. Bonus points if you can play with multiple mediums such as gifs and videos. Keep updating your posts regularly by adding new information and tags to keep search engine spiders happy.

One tip to follow for making your content more exhaustive is to look at how you can beat high-ranking posts for different keywords. For instance, if a high-ranking blog post is titled "20 cheapest travel destinations to visit this summer" do some more digging and come up with an even more exhaustive list of "30 cheapest summer travel destinations."

Include infographics and videos if you can to make it even more detailed. Great content is your most fool-proof armor when it comes to the great Google ranking battle.

Place RSS or other feed subscription buttons conspicuously on your posts to offer visitors the chance to subscribe to blog posts through email. This gives your blog readers immediate access to your newest posts frequently without having to keep visiting your blog/site for fresh content.

In an online world replete with several search engine algorithms that are designed to rank valuable and high-quality content, it is important to create a solid content strategy for long-term profitability. Become the one-stop trusted resource for information on several topics within your niche.

When you give visitors insights that equip them with actionable take-backs, they are more prepared to make informed buying decisions. You will invariably become a trusted resource when you aid their buying decisions positively. What's more? They will even go on to share their positive experience with you within their circle.

7. Ensure your blog is optimized for smartphone users. More than half the traffic on the internet comes from handheld devices. If you aren't using an optimized theme, you're leaving a lot of money on the table. Search engines use a variety of factors, including speed, browsing compatibility, user experience etc for ranking your page on search results. Responsiveness is an important factor when it comes to organically ranking pages on Google.

The overall speed across devices is also an important factor when it comes to Search Engine Optimization. Invest in tools that boost your blog/site speed and improve the overall user experience.

A simple tip such as using an image compression tool like Smush.it can help your blog/site achieve the perfect speed.

8. Stay away from cheap automated or other link building services that can hit your blog. Invest in gathering high-quality links of high PR (Page Rank) sites. Avoid spam like mass directory submissions and try to bag as many guest blogging opportunities as you can to link back to your blog. Also, keyword-stuffed content created using automated tools is heavily looked down upon by Google.

9. Once you've done your keyword research and unearthed unique gems, place them naturally within the blog posts to please both your readers and web crawlers responsible for indexing it. Include your keywords in the following places for maximum effectiveness – Title, Title tags, meta description, heading and subheadings, introductory sentence, final paragraph and anchor text (the hyperlink used to link to other posts/pages on your site).

It's no secret that the big G loves long posts so keep your posts as long and detailed as possible with lots of subheadings, bullet points, signal words (firstly, secondly, consequently) and white space between paragraphs. Posts should be a minimum of 300 words. Though it will vary based on your strategy, a keyword density of 1 to 2 percent is ideal. For instance, for a 300-word blog piece, use keywords not more than 3- 6 times.

Also, it is a good practice to use only one or two keywords/key phrases per blog post. Excess keywords can end up diluting your blog content, and start appearing spammy not just to search engines but also your readers. Try and maximize your organic traffic by including more long tail keywords.

10. Use the Yoast SEO plugin. Yoast is a must-include plugin for those relying heavily on organic search engine traffic. It

helps you create SEO friendly posts. Among other handy functions, the plug-in allows you to formulate an optimized meta description, analyzes your article for readability, checks for links within the post and calculates the post's keyword density.

The plug-in gives you an overall score based on a green dot on several parameters. If you score a green on most factors with a few red dots, you can bag a "good" score.

11. Structure your blog post efficiently by using lots of headings and subheadings. They're vital for both – Search Engine Optimization as well as readability. Headings give Google's web crawlers a helpful indication about the primary topic covered in a lengthy post, which can invariably impact on your placement rank.

If you want to improve the overall readability of the post make it effortless for readers to find their way through the pile of content. Make your content more scan-able by utilizing subheadings (good place for using keywords, though don't use a keyword in every sub-heading).

Conclusion

Thank you for downloading my book, Affiliate

The Complete Guide to *Affiliate Marketing (How to Make Money Online Selling Other People's Products).*

I sincerely hope this book provides you with several proven, actionable and little-known insights about profiting from selling other people's products and services.

The next step is to stop building six-figure castles in the air, and start taking action. No amount of information will ever be useful until you decide to use it.

Start applying these definitive affiliate marketing principles right away and learn on your journey to profitability.

Lastly, if you enjoyed reading the book, please take some time out to share your opinion by posting a review on Amazon. It'd be highly appreciated.

Here's to your success as an affiliate marketer!

www.ingramcontent.com/pod-product-compliance
Lightning Source LLC
Chambersburg PA
CBHW071250170526
45165CB00003B/1289